MW01504617

THE ULTIMATE GOLDEN STATE WARRIORS BOOK FOR KIDS AND TEENS

160+ Fun, Surprising, And Educational Stories And Trivia Quizzes About Players And History

John Stevenson

ISBN 9798340750273

Contents

CHAPTER ONE: The Beginning: 6

Golden State Warriors Early Years

CHAPTER TWO: Famous Rivalries 11

CHAPTER THREE: Legendary Players 20

Stephen Curry 21

Wilt Chamberlain 26

Rick Barry 29

Kevin Durant 33

Tim Hardaway 37

Chris Mullin 40

Klay Thompson   44

Nate Thurmond   47

CHAPTER FOUR: Coaches And Their   65
Impact

CHAPTER FIVE: Memorable Moments   73
in Warriors History: Championship Wins,
Historic Games, And Record-Breaking
Performances

CHAPTER SIX: Fun Facts and Trivia: 88
Did You Know, Nicknames, And Pop Culture

BONUS QUIZ! More Golden State Warriors   93
Questions!

CHAPTER ONE

The Beginning: Golden State Warriors Early Years

The Golden State Warriors are one of the most successful basketball teams in NBA history. The team was formed in 1946 by a man named Peter A. Tyrrell.

But, the Golden State Warriors weren't called the Golden State Warriors for their first 25 years. They were the Philadelphia Warriors then San Francisco Warriors! The team started in Philadelphia as part of the Basketball Association of

America. However, in 1962, Tyrrell decided to move the team to San Francisco, so they got a new name: the San Francisco Warriors. In 1971, the team had another name change. This time, the name was changed to the current Golden State Warriors.

The Basketball Association of America later merged with the National Basketball League (NBL) to form the NBA. The Warriors became one of 17 teams to join the new NBA.

They made history right away, too. The Warriors won the very first NBA Finals in 1947, defeating the Chicago Stags 4-1. They were led by Joe Fulks, who was the top scorer that season. He averaged 23.2 points per game. That is almost seven points more than anyone else!

Building a great team wasn't easy. It took years of hard work, strategy, and a "never give up" attitude to make the Warriors a respected team.

After winning their third title in 1975, the team had to wait 40 years for another chance at the Finals. But in 2014-15, their dynasty began as the team won four of the next eight NBA titles. Star players such as Stephen Curry and Andre Iguodala were key to the Warriors' success.

From their early days as the Philadelphia Warriors to winning multiple-time championships, the Golden State Warriors have truly earned their place in NBA history.

CHAPTER ONE QUIZ

1. What year were the Golden State Warriors founded?

a. 1945

b. 1946

c. 1947

d. 1948

2. Who founded the Golden State Warriors?

a. Tony Ressler

b. Walter A. Brown

c. Abe Saperstein

d. Peter A. Tyrrell

3. What was the name of the league the Golden State Warriors played in before the NBA?

a. America Basketball Association league

b. Basketball America league

c. Basketball Association league

d. Basketball Association of America league

4. Which year was the team's name changed to the Golden State Warriors?

a. 1962

b. 1967

c. 1970

d. 1971

5. Which team did the Warriors defeat to win the very first NBA Finals in 1947?

a. Chicago Stags

b. Pittsburgh Ironmen

c. New York Knicks

d. Boston Celtics

6. Who was the team's top scorer in 1947, averaging 23.2 points per game?

a. Jack George

b. George Dempsey

c. Joe Fulks

d. Tom Gola

7. How many different names did the team have before becoming the Golden State Warriors?

a. 1

b. 2

c. 3

d. 4

Quiz Answers

1. 1946 **2.** Peter A. Tyrrell **3.** Basketball Association of America league **4.** 1971 **5.** Chicago Stags **6.** Joe Fulks **7.** 2

CHAPTER TWO

Famous Rivalries

As the Golden State Warriors became one of the most successful NBA teams, many major rivals look to defeat the Warriors every time they meet.

Here are three of the Warriors' fiercest rivals, whose intense matchups have produced some of the most exciting and memorable moments in NBA history.

Cleveland Cavaliers

The Warriors and Cavaliers rivalry is one of the most popular in the NBA. These two teams' rivalry is so strong and well-known that every game between them is intense to watch!

The Warriors met LeBron James and the Cavaliers in the finals four straight times between 2015 and 2018. The Warriors won three of those four matchups.

LeBron James was the best player in the league, but he had a tough time beating the Warriors. Golden State had one of the strongest teams in the NBA back then.

The Warriors made a huge move after the Cavaliers won the 2016 NBA Finals in a close 4-3 series. They signed Kevin Durant, another star player. With Durant's amazing shooting skills, the Warriors became known as a "super-team."

With Durant and Stephen Curry leading the Warriors, they got their revenge in the 2017 NBA Finals. They defeated the Cavaliers 4-1.

After LeBron James left the Cavaliers, the rivalry has died down a bit. Still, there's still a long, rooted history between these two clubs. Fans still remember those intense games. The rivalry is alive, even if things have calmed down for now.

Los Angeles Clippers

At first, the Warriors couldn't beat the Clippers, no matter how hard they tried.

Back in 2014, Golden State Warriors faced the Los Angeles Clippers in the second round of the playoffs.

The Warriors were still a young, up-and-coming team. Stephen Curry and his teammates played hard, but the Clippers won the series in six games.

The Clippers had a powerhouse trio: Blake Griffin, Chris Paul, and DeAndre Jordan. They were just too strong for the young Dubs at the time.

But things began to change the very next year. The script flipped. Suddenly, the Clippers couldn't keep up with the Warriors!

From the 2014-15 season onward, the Warriors became a force to be reckoned with. The sharpshooting of Curry and Klay Thompson caused all kinds of problems for the Clippers.

The tables had turned, and the Warriors started winning. They proved they had become one of the best teams in the NBA.

Houston Rockets

The rivalry between the Warriors and the Rockets was one of the biggest in the NBA from 2015 to 2019.

In four of the Warriors' five trips to the finals during that time, they had to go through the Rockets first. Even though the Warriors always managed to win, it was never an easy battle.

The most intense showdown between the two teams happened in 2018.

That year, the Rockets had a 3-2 series lead. They were only one win away from knocking out the Warriors. But the Warriors didn't give up. They fought back and won the next two games to make it to the finals.

Since then, the Rockets haven't been able to beat the Warriors. But every game between these two teams has been full of excitement and unforgettable moments. Whenever the Warriors play the Rockets, you know it's going to be a thrilling game.

CHAPTER TWO QUIZ

1. How many times did the Warriors defeat the Cavaliers in the finals between 2015 and 2018?

a. 1 time

b. 2 times

c. 3 times

d. 4 times

2. Which year did the Warriors lose to the Cavaliers in the finals?

a. 2015

b. 2016

c. 2017

d. 2018

3. What was the score of the 2017 NBA Finals between the Cleveland Cavaliers and Golden State Warriors?

a. 3-1

b. 4-1

c. 2-2

d. 1-3

4. Who were the two players that helped the Warriors beat the Clippers starting in the 2014-15 season?

a. Draymond Green and Andre Iguodala

b. Stephen Curry and Klay Thompson

c. Shaun Livingston and Justin Holiday

d. Harrison Barnes and Andrew Bogut

Quiz Answers

1. 3 times **2.** 2016 **3.** 4-1 **4.** Stephen Curry and Klay Thompson

CHAPTER THREE

Legendary Players

The Golden State Warriors have some of the greatest players to ever step onto a basketball court. Since the beginning of the NBA, the Warriors have produced many Hall of Famers.

These famous Warriors players have shown what it means to play for the Dubs, whether they are winning championships or making amazing dunks.

STEPHEN CURRY

**4X NBA CHAMPION
(2015, 2017, 2018, 2022)**

2X NBA MVP

10X NBA ALL-STAR

4X ALL-NBA FIRST TEAM

BORN
March 14, 1988
Akron, Ohio, U.S.

POSITION
Forward/Guard

NBA DRAFT
2009 / round: 1 /
pick: 7

Stephen Curry is one of the greatest players ever to wear a Golden State Warriors jersey. He's known as the best shooter in the NBA, famous for making incredible three-point shots. Since joining the Warriors in 2009, Steph has won four championships. He has earned multiple Most Valuable Player (MVP) awards.

But did you know that basketball runs in his family? Steph's dad, Dell Curry, was also a famous NBA player for the Charlotte Hornets.

As a kid, Steph spent a lot of time watching his dad's games and meeting legendary basketball stars. It might have been easy for him to think he didn't need to work hard. But, Steph knew that if he wanted to be like his dad, he had to practice a lot.

After school, Steph would head to the backyard and practice shooting for hours. One day, his dad noticed Steph's shot was easy to block. One summer afternoon, Dell watched Steph practicing in the backyard. He noticed something off about his son's form.

"Steph, come here for a second," Dell called out. "Your shot's too easy to block. Let's work on that."

For the entire summer, father and son worked tirelessly on Steph's shooting technique. "Higher, Steph! Release it higher!" Dell would shout, mimicking a defender's outstretched arms.

Steph kept playing throughout high school, but one thing was holding him back: his height.

As a senior, Steph was about six feet tall, much shorter than the average NBA player, who is around 6'6". Scouts doubted his ability because he was smaller and skinnier than other players.

Steph knew he had to adjust his shooting style to release the ball higher. That way, he could avoid getting blocked by taller opponents.

Still, many college scouts didn't believe he had what it took to play at the next level.

"You've got a good shot, but you're too small. You'll never make it in the big leagues," a scout had said.

"I might be too short or skinny right now," Steph replied, "but I'm not going to let that stop me from reaching the NBA."

Steph decided to attend Davidson College, where he quickly became a basketball sensation. In his freshman year, he broke the NCAA record for three-pointers by a rookie! By his sophomore year, he had grown to 6'2". By the time he left college after his junior year, he was the top scorer in the country.

In 2009, Steph was drafted seventh overall by the Warriors. Coach Don Nelson knew Steph's quick shooting and agility would fit perfectly with his fast-paced system called "Nellie Ball."

Steph didn't disappoint. He became the Warriors' starting point guard and averaged 17.5 points per game in his rookie season. He wowed fans with his long-range shooting.

Over the next two seasons, Steph led the league in three-pointers made. In 2015, he helped the Warriors win their first NBA title in 40 years. He then went on to win three more championships in 2017, 2018, and 2022.

Steph Curry went from being an underrated high school player to one of the greatest players in history. He has shown that hard work and perseverance can help you rise above any challenge. Never judge a book by its cover, because what's inside can change the game!

WILT CHAMBERLAIN

2X NBA CHAMPION (1967, 1972)

4X NBA MVP

13X NBA ALL-STAR

7X ALL-NBA FIRST TEAM

BORN
August 21, 1936
Philadelphia,
Pennsylvania, U.S.

POSITION
Center

NBA DRAFT
1959: territorial
pick

Can you imagine scoring 100 points in a single basketball game? Well, that's exactly what Wilt Chamberlain did on March 2, 1962.

The Philadelphia Warriors were playing against the New York Knicks. Wilt led his team to a 169-147 victory. This incredible achievement happened in just his third year in the league.

Wilt was no ordinary basketball player. He was an unstoppable offensive force and became one of the greatest players to ever play the game. He joined the Warriors in 1959 and quickly earned the Rookie of the Year award.

During the 1961-62 season, Wilt set another record that might never be broken. He scored an unbelievable 4,029 points in the regular season. He became the only player to ever score more than 4,000 points in a single season. On average, that was an incredible 50.4 points per game.

What made Wilt special wasn't just his scoring. He could outjump anyone, with a vertical leap of 54 inches. That's as tall as a 12-year-old kid. His leaping ability made it look like he was flying over defenders.

And he wasn't just tall. Wilt was one of the fastest players of his time. As a former track and field athlete, he could outrun nearly everyone on the court. This was amazing for someone who stood 7'1".

In 1962, Wilt and the Warriors moved to San Francisco. There, he led the league in scoring for the next two seasons.

In 1965, Wilt was traded to the Philadelphia 76ers. By the time he retired in 1973, he had become the all-time leader in career points with 31,419.

Wilt's dominance even caused changes to the NBA's rules. They widened the lane to make it harder for big men like him to score near the basket. They also banned dunking during free throws. They made it illegal to inbound the ball over the backboard, because Wilt would leap from the foul line and put the ball in the basket.

Wilt Chamberlain's impact on basketball was so huge that the game changed because of him.

RICK BARRY

1X NBA CHAMPION (1975)

1X NBA FINALS MVP

8X NBA ALL-STAR

5X ALL-NBA FIRST TEAM

BORN
March 28, 1944
Elizabeth, New
Jersey, U.S.

POSITION
Small forward

NBA DRAFT
1965 / round: 1 /
pick: 2

Rick Barry was known for two things: his unusual way of shooting free throws and his fiery competitiveness. He wasn't afraid to speak his mind and could be tough to get along with. But, on the court, he was a force to be reckoned with.

Rick's love for basketball started with his dad, who taught him how to shoot underhand.

"Remember, son," his dad called out, "underhanded is the way to go!"

Rick looked skeptical. "But Dad, nobody shoots like that anymore. It looks silly!"

His dad chuckled, "Sometimes, being different is what makes you great. Now, give it a try."

Reluctantly, Rick swung the ball between his legs and released it in a graceful arc. Swish! Nothing but net.

As Rick grew older, his unique shooting style became his trademark. By the time Rick was in fifth grade, he was already playing against middle school kids. His skills grew, and he became the NCAA Division I scoring champion at the University of Miami.

In 1965, Rick was drafted by the San Francisco Warriors as the second overall pick in the NBA Draft. During his rookie season, he was unstoppable. He averaged 25.7 points and 10 rebounds per game, which earned him the NBA Rookie of the Year Award.

By his second season, Rick was on fire! He scored a career-high 2,775 points and led the entire league with an average of 35.6 points per game. He also set an NBA record for free throws, all while shooting underhanded.

But not everyone was impressed. Fans began to grumble about his playing style. People said he was being selfish with the ball.

"Barry's a ball hog!" one fan shouted from the stands. "He needs to learn to share!"

In 1968, Rick left the Warriors to join the Oakland Oaks. After bouncing around a few teams, he returned to the Warriors in 1972 with a new approach. This time, he focused less on scoring and more on passing. When he wasn't making baskets, he was setting up plays with his creative passing.

Rick's greatest moment with the Warriors came in the 1975 NBA Finals. He led the team against the Washington Bullets and was named the Most Valuable Player of the series.

Rick left the Warriors for good in 1978 to join the Houston Rockets. In 1987, all of his hard work paid off when he was inducted into the Naismith Memorial Basketball Hall of Fame.

KEVIN DURANT

2X NBA CHAMPION (2017, 2018)

2X NBA FINALS MVP

14X NBA ALL-STAR

6X ALL-NBA FIRST TEAM

BORN
September 29, 1988
Washington, D.C.,
U.S.

POSITION
Power forward /
Small forward

NBA DRAFT
2007 / round: 1 /
pick: 2

33

Kevin Durant is considered one of the best basketball players in the world. But his journey started with some challenges. When Kevin was in middle school, he was unusually tall for his age. He was already six feet. Some kids made fun of him for being so tall. As he walked into class, he heard the familiar whispers.

"Look, it's the giant!" one kid snickered.

Kevin slumped into his seat, trying to make himself smaller. Later that day, he confided in his grandmother, Barbara.

"Grandma, why do I have to be so tall? Everyone makes fun of me," Kevin said, his voice cracking.

Barbara cupped his face in her hands. "Kevin, your height is a gift. One day, you'll see how it makes you perfect for basketball."

Her words stuck with him, fueling a dream that would soon take shape.

When Kevin was around ten, he told his mom he dreamed of becoming an NBA player. His mom, who was raising two boys alone, did everything she could to help him chase that dream. She made sure he stayed focused and practiced hard, even when times were tough.

In high school, Kevin grew even more. He grew an incredible seven inches to reach 6'9". His skills on the basketball court were just as impressive as his height. Top Division I colleges wanted him to play for them. Kevin, however, chose the University of Texas Longhorns in Austin. He wanted to make his own path.

As a Longhorn, Kevin dominated the court. He won several awards, including the College Player of the Year.

In 2007, he was drafted second overall by the Seattle SuperSonics, who would later become the Oklahoma City Thunder. He quickly proved his talent by winning the NBA Rookie of the Year Award.

After playing nine seasons with the Thunder, Kevin made a huge decision that shocked the NBA. He joined the Golden State Warriors in 2016. Some people criticized him for this, but Kevin knew what he was doing. It turned out to be a winning choice.

In June 2017, Kevin led the Warriors to victory in the NBA Finals against LeBron James and the Cleveland Cavaliers. His incredible scoring earned him the Finals MVP award.

The next year, he showed his leadership when Steph Curry suffered an injury. Kevin stepped up and carried his team through the early rounds of the playoffs. When Curry returned, the Warriors faced the Cavaliers again in the Finals. They defeated them again, and Kevin won his second straight Finals MVP.

In 2019, Kevin decided to leave the Warriors and join the Brooklyn Nets. Then, in 2023, he made another move to the Phoenix Suns. Through it all, Kevin Durant has shown that hard work and determination can turn a tall dream into an amazing reality.

TIM HARDAWAY

1X NBA ALL-ROOKIE FIRST TEAM

5X NBA ALL-STAR

1X ALL-NBA FIRST TEAM

BORN
September 1, 1966
Chicago, Illinois, U.S.

POSITION
Point guard

NBA DRAFT
1989 / round: 1 /
pick: 14

Tim Hardaway grew up on the South Side of Chicago in the 1970s, where life wasn't always easy. His neighborhood was tough, but Tim found a way to escape through basketball. He spent hours every day practicing and perfecting his game, dreaming of making it big one day.

Eventually, Tim moved to Texas to play college basketball at the University of Texas at El Paso (UTEP).

When he first arrived, he was a 5-foot-11 point guard who loved to run and gun. But, his shot wasn't exactly pretty. People used to say his shot looked like the Earth spinning sideways. But Tim didn't let that bother him.

While playing at UTEP, Tim worked hard on improving his skills. He created a signature move: the crossover dribble. This move became known as the "UTEP two-step."

It was like watching a bolt of lightning flash across the basketball court. In just a split second, Tim would dribble the ball left to right, then right to left. He would leave his defenders stuck in place, while he zoomed past them to the basket.

His college coach, Don Haskins, recognized his potential early on.

"Tim," he said during a particularly grueling practice, "that move of yours is going to make history. Keep working on it."

Tim's hard work paid off during the 1989 NBA Draft. He was selected by the Golden State Warriors with the 14th overall pick.

He played six exciting seasons for the Warriors, becoming one of their star players. Tim averaged 19.8 points, 9.3 assists, 3.6 rebounds, and 1.9 steals over 422 games. He also earned a spot in the NBA All-Star Game for three straight years.

One of Tim's greatest achievements was reaching 5,000 points and 2,500 assists faster than almost any other player in NBA history. He was known for being quick, smart, and unstoppable on the court.

Tim played for the Warriors until the middle of the 1995–96 season when he was traded to the Miami Heat. But, his time in Golden State is remembered as one of the best chapters of his career.

CHRIS MULLIN

5X NBA ALL-STAR

1X ALL-NBA FIRST TEAM

2X ALL-NBA SECOND TEAM

BORN
July 30, 1963
New York City,
New York, U.S.

POSITION
Small forward /
Shooting guard

NBA DRAFT
1985 / round: 1 /
pick: 7

Chris Mullin was just a kid from New York, but he loved basketball more than anything. He spent his days playing street ball games all over the city.

"Hey Chris, you gonna join us for some hoops?" his friends would call out.

"You know it!" Chris would reply, a grin spreading across his face as he jogged over to the court.

By the time he was in fourth grade, he had already won a national foul shooting contest. People could tell early on that Chris was something special.

As he grew up, Chris became a New York basketball legend. In high school, they called him "the gym rat." He was always working out in the gym, practicing his shots.

"Chris, it's late. Don't you want to go home?" his coach would ask, keys jingling in his hand.

"Just five more minutes, Coach," Chris would plead, sweat dripping from his brow. "I've almost got this new move down."

He kept the same work ethic in college, where he would often stay in the gym until well past midnight. Chris wasn't the tallest or the fastest player. But, he was one of the best shooters, thanks to his relentless practice.

There was even a time when a blizzard hit and snowed everyone in at school. While most people stayed inside to keep warm, there was the sound of a lone basketball bouncing in the gym.

"Chris? Is that you in there?" his roommate called out, peering through the gym doors.

"Yeah, it's me," Chris shouted back, not breaking his rhythm. "Figured I'd make the most of this snow day."

His roommate shook his head in disbelief. "Only you would think of a blizzard as extra practice time."

When the snow stopped, Chris stayed even longer, continuing to perfect his game.

In 1985, Chris entered the NBA draft. He was selected seventh overall by the Golden State Warriors. He quickly made a name for himself as a sharp-shooting guard.

But when Coach Don Nelson came to the Warriors, he moved Chris to small forward. That's when Chris really started to shine.

From 1988 to 1993, Chris scored an average of 25 or more points and grabbed five rebounds each season. During those years, the Warriors made it to the playoffs five times in a row. Chris had finally become the star player the Warriors had hoped for when they drafted him.

Chris teamed up with Mitch Richmond. Together, they became the highest-scoring duo in the NBA, averaging a combined 48.6 points per game. They were also the youngest teammates to lead the league in scoring.

Chris kept getting better and better. In the 1991-92 season, he was named to the All-NBA First Team.

After playing for the Warriors for many years, Chris was traded to the Indiana Pacers after the 1996-97 season.

By the time he retired, he had played 16 seasons in the NBA. He scored more than 17,000 points and was a five-time All-Star. Chris Mullin will always be remembered as one of the hardest-working and best shooters the NBA has ever seen.

KLAY THOMPSON

4X NBA CHAMPION

5X NBA ALL-STAR

1X NBA THREE-POINT CONTEST CHAMPION

1X NBA ALL-ROOKIE FIRST TEAM

BORN
February 8, 1990
Los Angeles,
California, U.S.

POSITION
Small forward /
Shooting guard

NBA DRAFT
2011 / round: 1 /
pick: 11

Growing up, Klay Thompson always looked up to his dad. His father, Mychal Thompson, was a two-time NBA champion who played for the Los Angeles Lakers. From a young age, Klay's dad taught him and his brother the importance of hard work and a love for basketball.

"Remember, boys," Mychal would say, tossing a ball to young Klay and his brother in their driveway. "Success doesn't come easy. It's all about the hours you put in when no one's watching."

By high school, Klay had developed a deadly jump shot and an incredible work ethic. In his senior year in 2008, he was averaging 21 points per game. He led his team to the Division 3 State Championship. In the finals, he set a new record for the most three-pointers made.

All the hours he spent in the gym, practicing his shot over and over again, paid off. As the final buzzer sounded, his teammates rushed to lift him onto their shoulders. Klay was named the Division 3 State Player of the Year.

The next big step for Klay was choosing where he would go to college. After thinking about it, he decided to attend Washington State University. As a freshman, he was named to the Pac-10 All-Freshman Team.

By his sophomore year, Klay was already known as a sharpshooter. He averaged 19.6 points per game and impressed everyone with his three-point skills.

In 2011, Klay declared for the NBA Draft. On draft night, his lifelong dream became a reality. He was selected 11th overall by the Golden State Warriors. It was just the beginning of his incredible NBA journey.

Klay quickly became one of the best shooters the game has ever seen. Teaming up with Stephen Curry, they formed the "Splash Brothers." They became the most dangerous shooting duo in NBA history. In the 2013 season, Klay and Steph made a combined 483 three-pointers. It was a record for the most ever by two teammates!

Klay's shooting helped lead the Warriors to four NBA championships. In 2016, he even won the NBA All-Star 3-point contest. He's widely known as one of the greatest three-point shooters of all time.

After 13 years with the Warriors, Klay made a big decision and joined the Dallas Mavericks in 2024. It starts a new chapter in his legendary career.

NATE THURMOND

7X NBA ALL-STAR

2X NBA ALL-DEFENSIVE FIRST TEAM

1X NBA ALL-ROOKIE FIRST TEAM

BORN
July 25, 1941
Akron, Ohio, U.S.

POSITION
Center / Power forward

NBA DRAFT
1963 / round: 1 / pick: 3

Nate Thurmond was one of the greatest NBA centers of all time. He was fast and had super long arms. He was a master at blocking shots and grabbing rebounds. Nate even holds the NBA record for the most rebounds in a single quarter! His tough, no-nonsense style of play scared even the best players in the league.

"Man, I hate going up against Nate," one player was overheard saying in the locker room. "It's like trying to score against an octopus with a bad attitude!"

In 1963, the San Francisco Warriors picked Nate as the third overall choice in the NBA Draft. In his rookie season, Nate learned from the best as Wilt Chamberlain's apprentice. Playing alongside such a legend helped Nate improve quickly. When Chamberlain was traded, Nate stepped into the spotlight as the team's main center.

With more time on the court, Nate's skills really began to shine. He averaged 16.5 points and 18.1 rebounds per game, numbers that made him a star.

However, Chamberlain's trade left the Warriors struggling. Their 1964-65 season ended with a tough 17-63 record.

Even though times were tough, Nate stayed positive. He always believed things would get better. By the 1966-67 season, the Warriors had bounced back, and Nate had become a steady All-Star. He played in three straight All-Star Games from 1965 to 1967, proving his skills on both ends of the court.

Nate's best season came in 1968-69, when he averaged 21.5 points and an incredible 19.7 rebounds per game.

Even though he wasn't the kind of player who did flashy dunks or tricky dribbles, he earned respect from his opponents. What mattered most to Nate was that his fellow players knew just how good he was.

They called him one of the best defensive big men in basketball. Many admired his hard work, consistency, and well-rounded game.

After an amazing 11 years with the Warriors, Nate was traded to the Chicago Bulls in 1974. During his time with the Warriors, he became the team's all-time leader in games played, rebounds, and minutes on the court.

CHAPTER THREE QUIZ

1. What is Stephen Curry most famous for in the NBA?

a. Most finals appearances

b. Making three-point shots

c. Tallest player in the NBA

d. Shortest player in the NBA

2. What is the name of Stephen Curry's dad?

a. Dell Curry

b. Bill Curry

c. James Curry

d. Michael Curry

3. Which college did Stephen Curry play for?

a. UCLA

b. University of San Francisco

c. Davidson College

d. Duke

4. Which year was Stephen Curry drafted by the Golden State Warriors?

a. 2000

b. 2003

c. 2006

d. 2009

5. What is Stephen Curry's Warriors jersey number?

a. 14

b. 17

c. 30

d. 45

6. What NCAA record did Stephen Curry break as a freshman in college?

a. Most free throws made

b. Most rebounds

c. Most blocked shots

d. Most three-pointers by a rookie

7. Which team did Wilt Chamberlain score 100 points against in 1962?

a. Los Angeles Lakers

b. Boston Celtics

c. Dallas Mavericks

d. New York Knicks

8. What position did Wilt Chamberlain play?

a. Small Forward

b. Point Guard

c. Center

d. Power Forward

9. Which year did Wilt Chamberlain join the Philadelphia Warriors?

a. 1956

b. 1957

c. 1958

d. 1959

10. How many NBA All-Star games did Wilt Chamberlain play in?

a. 10

b. 11

c. 12

d. 13

11. How many times did Wilt Chamberlain win the NBA MVP?

a. 4

b. 6

c. 8

d. 10

12. Which year was Wilt Chamberlain traded to the Philadelphia 76ers?

a. 1960

b. 1963

c. 1965

d. 1968

13. What was Rick Barry known for?

a. Being the fastest player in the NBA

b. His unusual way of shooting free throws

c. Most number of points scored in a game

d. Most number of consecutive games played

14. What position did Rick Barry play?

a. Small Forward

b. Point Guard

c. Center

d. Power Forward

15. Which year was Rick Barry drafted by the Golden State Warriors?

a. 1965

b. 1966

c. 1967

d. 1968

16. What award did Rick Barry win in his rookie year?

a. NBA Finals MVP

b. Clutch Player of the Year

c. NBA Rookie of the Year Award

d. Sixth Man of the Year

17. Which college did Rick Barry play for?

a. Ohio State University

b. Ohio University

c. Oberlin College

d. University of Miami

18. Why was Kevin Durant bullied in middle school?

a. He was unusually tall for his age

b. He did not like to play sports

c. He dressed differently from other kids

d. He was rowdy in school

19. Which NBA team did Kevin Durant play for before joining the Warriors?

a. Oklahoma City Thunder

b. Philadelphia 76ers

c. Toronto Raptors

d. Detroit Pistons

20. Which year did Kevin Durant join the Warriors?

a. 2014

b. 2015

c. 2016

d. 2017

21. Which year did Kevin Durant win his first Finals MVP award?

a. 2016

b. 2017

c. 2018

d. 2019

22. What position did Tim Hardaway play?

a. Small Forward

b. Point Guard

c. Center

d. Power Forward

23. What was the name of Tim Hardaway's signature move?

a. UTEP crossover

b. UTEP dribble

c. UTEP dunk

d. UTEP two-step

24. How many seasons did Tim Hardaway play for the Warriors?

a. 5 seasons

b. 6 seasons

c. 9 seasons

d. 11 seasons

25. Which college did Tim Hardaway play for?

a. University of Indiana

b. Indiana State

c. University of Texas at El Paso

d. Michigan State

26. How many seasons did Chris Mullin play in the NBA?

a. 10 seasons

b. 16 seasons

c. 19 seasons

d. 20 seasons

27. What contest did Chris Mullin win when he was in fourth grade?

a. A national foul shooting contest

b. A national three-point contest

c. A national rebound contest

d. A national dribbling contest

28. What nickname was Chris Mullin given in high school?

a. Sharp shooter

b. Hardworker

c. Gym rat

d. Three pointer

29. How many times was Chris Mullin an All-Star?

a. 2

b. 3

c. 4

d. 5

30. Which team was Chris Mullin traded to after the 1996-97 season?

a. Denver Nuggets

b. Indiana Pacers

c. Charlotte Hornets

d. Toronto Raptors

31. Which year was Chris Mullin named to the All-NBA First Team?

a. 1990

b. 1991

c. 1992

d. 1993

32. What record did Klay Thompson set during his high school's Division 3 State Championship finals?

a. Most assists made

b. Most steals made

c. Most three-pointers made

d. Most rebounds made

33. How many years did Klay Thompson play for the Warriors?

a. 10 years

b. 11 years

c. 12 years

d. 13 years

34. What nickname was given to the partnership between Klay Thompson and Stephen Curry?

a. Score Brothers

b. Splash Brothers

c. Shoot Brothers

d. Two Brothers

35. How many NBA championships did Klay Thompson win with the Golden State Warriors?

a. 2

b. 3

c. 4

d. 5

36. What record did Klay Thompson and Stephen Curry break in 2013?

a. Most combined three-pointers by two teammates

b. Most combined assists by two teammates

c. Most combined steals by two teammates

d. Most combined minutes played by two teammates

37. Which team was Klay Thompson traded to in 2024?

a. Atlanta Hawks

b. Brooklyn Nets

c. Sacramento Kings

d. Dallas Mavericks

38. What NBA contest did Klay Thompson win in 2016?

a. NBA All-Star Slam Dunk contest

b. NBA All-Star 3-point contest

c. NBA All-Star Skills contest

d. NBA Rising Stars Challenge

39. Who was Nate Thurmond's mentor when he first joined the team as a rookie?

a. Wilt Chamberlain

b. Wayne Hightower

c. Gary Hill

d. George Lee

40. How many years did Nate Thurmond play for the Warriors?

a. 11 years

b. 15 years

c. 17 years

d. 19 years

41. Which team was Nate Thurmond traded to in 1974?

a. Milwaukee Bucks

b. Miami Heat

c. Chicago Bulls

d. Orlando Magic

Quiz Answers

1. Making three-point shots **2.** Dell Curry **3.** Davidson College **4.** 2009 **5.** 30 **6.** Most three-pointers by a rookie **7.** New York Knicks **8.** Center **9.** 1959 **10.** 13 NBA All-Star games **11.** 4 times **12.** 1965 **13.** His unusual way of shooting free throws **14.** Small Forward **15.** 1965 **16.** NBA Rookie of the Year Award **17.** University of Miami **18.** He was unusually tall for his age **19.** Oklahoma City Thunder **20.** 2016 **21.** 2017 **22.** Point Guard **23.** UTEP two-step **24.** 6 seasons **25.** University of Texas at El Paso **26.** 16 seasons **27.** A national foul shooting contest **28.** Gym rat **29.** 5 times **30.** Indiana Pacers **31.** 1992 **32.** Most three-pointers made **33.** 13 years **34.** Splash Brothers **35.** 4 championships **36.** Most combined three-pointers by two teammates **37.** Dallas Mavericks **38.** NBA All-Star 3-point contest **39.** Wilt Chamberlain **40.** 11 years **41.** Chicago Bulls

CHAPTER FOUR

Coaches And Their Impact

Behind every great basketball team is a visionary coach who inspires players and creates a winning culture. During the Golden State Warriors' long history, many legendary coaches have guided the team through championships and challenges from the sidelines.

Coach Steve Kerr is the greatest coach in the history of the Golden State Warriors. He joined the Warriors in 2014 as the team's 25th head coach. From the very start, he made a huge impact.

Coach Kerr led the Warriors to five straight NBA Finals in his first five seasons. In his first season in 2015, he coached the Warriors to their first NBA Championship since 1975.

The next year, he led them to a record-breaking season. They won 73 games and only lost 9, setting an all-time NBA best regular season record.

Coach Kerr didn't stop there. He guided the Warriors to back-to-back championships in 2017 and 2018.

One of the reasons Coach Kerr has been so successful is because he was once one of the best three-point shooters in NBA history. He played for legendary teams like the Chicago Bulls and San Antonio Spurs. He learned from some of the greatest coaches like Phil Jackson and Gregg Popovich.

Coach Kerr brought new strategies and ideas that he learned from his playing days. He encouraged young players, like Stephen Curry, to grow. He allowed them to learn from their mistakes. With each game, their confidence and skills grew. The Warriors became stronger as a team.

In 2022, Coach Kerr added another championship to his legacy. He led the Warriors to victory over the Boston Celtics 4-2. This marked his fourth championship as head coach!

Another Golden State Warriors coach who left a lasting impact was Coach Don Nelson. He coached the Warriors twice. He first coached the team from 1988 to 1995. Then, he returned to coach the team again from 2006 to 2010.

Coach Nelson was known for his creative and innovative style of basketball. He came up with a unique strategy called "Nellie Ball." It was all about speeding up the game.

Instead of relying on big, tall players, he focused on smaller, quicker athletes. He wanted to use their speed and shooting ability to score points fast. That way, his team could overwhelm traditional defenses.

This strategy helped create the concept of the "point forward." It is a position where a taller player can handle the ball and lead the offense. That is something every team uses today!

Coach Nelson's creativity didn't always lead to championships, but it did leave a huge mark on the game. Over his 31 seasons as a coach, he earned 1,335 regular season wins. He was the all-time leader in regular season victories for a while.

Even though he didn't win many titles with his strategies, Coach Nelson changed the way basketball is played.

Today, teams everywhere embrace speed, shooting, and versatility. They all look for big players who can move and play fast.

CHAPTER FOUR QUIZ

1. Which year did Coach Steve Kerr join the Warriors?

a. 2012

b. 2013

c. 2014

d. 2015

2. How many championships has Coach Steve Kerr won with the Warriors?

a. 1

b. 2

c. 3

d. 4

3. How many games did Coach Steve Kerr win in his second year with the Warriors?

a. 70 games

b. 73 games

c. 76 games

d. 79 games

4. How many times was Coach Don Nelson hired as the Golden State Warriors' coach?

a. 1

b. 2

c. 3

d. 4

5. What was the name of Coach Don Nelson's innovative basketball strategy?

a. Nellie Ball

b. Point Guard

c. Nelson Point

d. Fast Forward

6. What special accomplishment did Coach Don Nelson achieve during his coaching career?

a. All-time leader in awards won

b. All-time leader in regular season losses

c. All-time leader in championship wins

d. All-time leader in regular season victories

Quiz Answers

1. 2014 **2.** 4 championships **3.** 73 games **4.** 2 times **5.** Nellie Ball **6.** All-time leader in regular season victories

CHAPTER FIVE

Memorable Moments in Warriors' History

The Golden State Warriors have had some amazing moments that fans will never forget. From winning the NBA Championship in 1975 to special moments like Stephen Curry's famous 54-point game in 2013, here are five exciting and unforgettable moments in Warriors history.

1975 NBA CHAMPIONSHIP

The 1975 NBA Championship was one of the most exciting moments in Golden State Warriors history. Back then, no one thought the Warriors had much of a chance to win it all.

The team had lost key players like Nate Thurmond. Their lineup was a mix of young, inexperienced guys, and older veterans. No one thought the Warriors had much of a chance to win it all.

In the locker room before their first playoff game, coach Al Attles looked at his ragtag group of players.

"Listen up, fellas," he said, his voice steady and determined. "I don't care what they're saying out there. We're not here to meet their expectations. We're here to shatter them."

The Warriors entered the playoffs as the underdogs. They fought tooth and nail through the Western Conference. Their leader was Rick Barry. He was a fierce competitor with a never-give-up attitude that bordered on obsession.

Rick had just finished an amazing season, and he was determined to guide this scrappy team to victory. His intensity was infectious, spreading through the team like wildfire.

When the Warriors made it to the Finals, they had to face the tough Washington Bullets. Each game was a nail-biter, with tensions running high both on and off the court.

Adding to the drama was Rick Barry's personal feud with some of the Bullets players. They thought he was arrogant, but Rick wasn't about to change his ways for anyone. He played with fire and confidence, and it made things even more exciting.

"You think I'm arrogant?" Rick scoffed when a reporter brought it up. "I'm not here to make friends. I'm here to win championships."

Rick was the star of the series, no question about it. He averaged 29.5 points, 5 assists, and 4 rebounds per game. Whether he was shooting free throws or dishing out passes, Rick led the Warriors to victory after victory.

His best game came in Game 3, when he scored 38 points. It helped his team stay ahead, even though the Bullets fought back hard. It was like a battle of wills. In the end, Rick's determination won out.

Finally, in Game 4, the Warriors won. It was the Warriors' first championship since 1956, back when the team was still in Philadelphia!

It was a thrilling victory that nobody saw coming. It remains one of the most dramatic titles in Warriors history.

WE BELIEVE WARRIORS UPSET THE MAVERICKS (2007)

Back in 2007, one of the most amazing stories in NBA playoff history took place. The "We Believe" Warriors pulled off one of the most unbelievable wins ever. They shocked everyone by beating the top-seeded Dallas Mavericks in the first round of the Western Conference playoffs.

The Warriors had to fight hard just to make it into the playoffs. No one thought they had any chance against the mighty Mavs, who had one of the best regular season records that year.

For 12 long years, the Warriors hadn't made the playoffs. They were stuck in losing seasons and didn't seem to have much hope of turning things around.

But their head coach, Don Nelson, believed in them. He told his players, "You know, we're gonna beat Dallas."

Coach Nelson knew the Mavericks well. After all, he had coached them for eight years. He had a plan to stop their star player, Dirk Nowitzki, who was the league's MVP that season. Coach Nelson decided to put smaller, faster defenders on Dirk. It would make it tough for him to get into a rhythm and score.

The Warriors believed in Coach Nelson's strategy and went into Game 1 with confidence. And guess what? They won! After that, they just kept rolling.

The fans were pumped, all wearing their "We Believe" T-shirts, and they were louder than ever. Every basket the Warriors made sent the crowd into a frenzy.

Even though the Mavericks fought back and won Game 5, the Warriors came home and crushed them in Game 6. The final score was Warriors 111, Mavericks 86.

The 2006-07 Warriors didn't just pull off an upset. They made history with one of the biggest surprises the NBA had ever seen.

STEPHEN CURRY'S 54-POINT GAME (2013)

Steph Curry had already shown a lot of promise in the early years of his NBA career. But he didn't become a true superstar until one unforgettable night. That night, he scored 54 points against the New York Knicks.

It was February 27, 2013, and the Warriors were playing the Knicks at Madison Square Garden.

At the time, Steph was averaging a decent 17.5 points per game. It was not bad, but not superstar level. Nobody knew he was about to become one of the greatest players of all time. He was still trying to prove he belonged with the NBA's elite.

Now, Madison Square Garden is special. It's often called the "Mecca of Basketball," where legends are made. Every player dreams of having a big game there.

And on that night, Curry's performance was nothing short of legendary. From the very start, you could tell something amazing was happening. He started draining deep three-pointers right away, and the Knicks couldn't stop him. No matter what they tried, Curry was on fire.

He put on a shooting show like no one had ever seen, sinking contested shots from way beyond the three-point line. His ball-handling was dazzling. He weaved through defenders and creating space to get off his shot. It was like magic. Every time Curry touched the ball, something incredible happened.

By the end of the game, Curry had racked up 54 points. He hit 18 of his 28 shots, including a jaw-dropping 11-of-13 from three-point range.

He didn't miss a single free throw either, going a perfect 7-for-7. He even led the team in assists with seven and grabbed three steals.

The Knicks tried three different players to guard him, but none of them could keep up. Curry's quick release and his deep range forced the Knicks to defend him beyond the three-point line. But even then, he kept finding ways to score with incredible accuracy.

Even though the Knicks ended up winning the game, that night was a turning point for Steph Curry and the Warriors. It was the moment Curry's true potential was revealed. It set the stage for the Warriors' dominant run to five straight NBA Finals from 2014 to 2019.

And it all started on that magical evening at Madison Square Garden, where Steph Curry's legend was born.

2015 NBA CHAMPIONSHIP – START OF A DYNASTY

The year was 2010. The Golden State Warriors had just finished another disappointing season. Before the Warriors became a four-time champion, the team had gone through years of struggle.

In the locker room after their final game, a young Stephen Curry sat with his head in his hands.

"We can't keep going on like this," he muttered to himself. "Something's got to change."

Little did Curry know, change was already in motion. The journey to the 2015 title began years earlier with some careful team building.

First, the Warriors made key moves in the NBA Draft. In 2009, they selected Stephen Curry. Then in 2011, they drafted Klay Thompson, followed by Draymond Green in 2012. These three players would soon become the heart and soul of the team.

But they couldn't do it alone. Enter Andre Iguodala and Andrew Bogut, veterans who brought grit and experience to the young squad.

It wasn't just about getting the right players, though. The Warriors also made a game-changing decision by hiring Steve Kerr as their head coach. Kerr brought new ideas and a fresh style of play. He helped unleash the full potential of Curry, Thompson, and Green.

From 2015 to 2016, the Warriors became a nightmare for other teams. They had one of the most unstoppable offenses in

NBA history. Most teams could handle stopping one superstar. But trying to stop three scoring machines was nearly impossible.

"How do you guard all of them?" one exasperated coach asked his staff during a timeout. "You take away Curry, Thompson burns you. You focus on those two, and Green picks you apart."

Over the course of three seasons, the Warriors won an incredible 207 games. They were also the first team in NBA history to make 1,000 three-pointers in a single season!

The Warriors set the standard for modern basketball with their "small-ball" lineup. They put Draymond Green at center and surrounded him with sharpshooters. It created a fast, high-scoring style of play that other teams couldn't keep up with.

The 2015 championship was just the beginning. But, it laid the groundwork for an era of dominance.

WARRIORS SILENCE THE THUNDER IN GAME 7 (2016)

On May 30, 2016, the Golden State Warriors pulled off an unforgettable win in Game 7. They beat the Oklahoma City Thunder 96-88 in the Western Conference Finals. This game became one of the most exciting and dramatic playoff series in NBA history.

It all started with the Thunder winning Game 1. But, the Warriors quickly responded by stealing Game 2 at home. With the series tied 1-1, the Thunder took charge, winning Games 3 and 4. The Warriors were now in a tough spot.

Down 3-1, the Warriors faced a must-win situation in Game 5. It was do-or-die situation. Many doubted whether the Warriors could bounce back after two crushing losses. But the Warriors had something special the Thunder didn't: an MVP named Stephen Curry.

As the Warriors huddled in the locker room before Game 5, Coach Steve Kerr's voice rang out, "We're not done yet. We've got a lot of fight left in us. Who says we can't make history?"

Steph Curry, his eyes blazing with determination, stood up. "Coach is right. We didn't come this far to go home now. Let's shock the world."

The Warriors fought hard, with Curry and Klay Thompson leading the way. Their defense also locked down the Thunder. The Warriors won Game 5, keeping their championship hopes alive and sending the series to Game 6.

Game 6 turned out to be one of the most iconic games in NBA history. The Warriors were back in Oklahoma City, where the crowd was loud. It seemed like this would be the night the Thunder would head to the NBA Finals. But Klay had other plans.

In one of the clutchest shooting displays ever, Klay scored 41 points. He kept hitting one big shot after another. The Warriors won 108-101, tying the series at 3-3 and forcing a Game 7 back in Oakland.

With the series all tied up, everything came down to Game 7. And this time, Stephen Curry took the spotlight. The reigning MVP put up 36 points. He dazzled with his ball-handling and timely shots that crushed the Thunder's spirit. Curry's performance was too much for Oklahoma City to handle. When the final buzzer sounded, the Warriors completed their epic comeback.

The Warriors' rally from a 3-1 deficit was a heartbreaking loss for the Thunder. But for the Warriors, it became one of the most thrilling playoff series in NBA history.

CHAPTER FIVE QUIZ

1. Who was the standout star of the 1975 NBA Championship?

a. Jamaal Wilkes

b. Rick Barry

c. Butch Beard

d. Clifford Ray

2. Which team did the Golden State Warriors defeat to win the 1975 NBA Championship?

a. St. Louis Hawks

b. Los Angeles Lakers

c. Washington Bullets

d. Detroit Falcons

3. Which team did the "We Believe" Warriors play against in the first round of the 2007 Western Conference playoffs?

a. Los Angeles Lakers

b. San Antonio Spurs

c. Dallas Mavericks

d. Atlanta Hawks

4. Who was the head coach of the 2007 "We Believe" Warriors?

a. Don Nelson

b. Steve Kerr

c. Al Attles

d. Mark Jackson

5. In which famous stadium did Steph Curry score 54 points against the New York Knicks?

a. TD Garden

b. Madison Square Garden

c. State Farm Arena

d. Barclays Center

6. Which team did the Warriors defeat in the 2016 Western Conference Finals?

a. Chicago Bulls

b. Boston Celtics

c. Los Angeles Lakers

d. Oklahoma City Thunder

Quiz Answers

1. Rick Barry **2.** Washington Bullets **3.** Dallas Mavericks **4.** Don Nelson **5.** Madison Square Garden **6.** Oklahoma City Thunder

CHAPTER SIX

Fun Facts and Trivia: Did You Know, Nicknames, And Pop Culture

The Golden State Warriors are one of only three teams that were part of the original NBA that's still around.

The Warriors are called the "Dubs." The nickname comes from shortening "Warriors" to the letter "W," and then shortening it even more to "Dubs."

The Warriors used to have a mascot called "Thunder." But they had to get rid of him when the Seattle SuperSonics moved and became the Oklahoma City Thunder.

When the team relocated from Philadelphia to San Francisco in 1962, they played their home games at the iconic Cow Palace. In 1971, they moved to the Oracle Arena in Oakland. They stayed there for 47 years. Today, the Warriors play at Chase Center in San Francisco.

The Golden State Warriors have won three MVP awards. Wilt Chamberlain won the award in 1959-60. Stephen Curry won the award in both 2014-15 and 2015-16.

The Warriors have retired six jerseys: Wilt Chamberlain (13), Tom Meschery (14), Al Attles (16), Chris Mullin (17), Rick Barry (24), and Nate Thurmond (42).

The all-time franchise leader in points is Stephen Curry. As of 2024, he has scored 23,668 points. The second highest scorer is Wilt Chamberlain, who scored 17,783 points.

The record for the most points scored in a single game by a Warriors player is held by Wilt Chamberlain, who scored 100 points against the New York Knicks on March 2, 1962.

The partnership between Stephen Curry and Klay Thompson is affectionately called the "Splash Brothers." This duo has completely changed the game of three-point shooting! With their amazing skills, they can make long-range shots like it's no big deal.

The Golden State Warriors have a loyal and passionate fan base that has supported the team through thick and thin. The fans are known as the "Dub Nation."

The longest winning streak in Warriors history is 28 games. Their streak ended when they were defeated by the Milwaukee Bucks on December 12, 2015.

Stephen Curry's real name is Wardell Stephen Curry II. He was named after his father. Even though he is widely known as "Stephen" or "Steph," his close friends still refer to him by his birth name.

Stephen Curry once starred in a Burger King commercial as a kid. In the commercial, his dad gave Steph advice on becoming a great basketball player. One of his signature lines was "bring home the bacon dad!"

HERE ARE MORE QUESTIONS TO TEST YOUR KNOWLEDGE OF THE GOLDEN STATE WARRIORS!

1. Which team did the Warriors defeat to win the 2018 NBA Championship?

a. Cleveland Cavaliers

b. Miami Heat

c. Boston Celtics

d. Houston Rockets

2. What colors are featured on the Warriors' home uniforms?

a. Red and white

b. Blue and gold

c. Green and yellow

d. Black and orange

3. Which Warriors player has the nickname "Iggy"?

a. Klay Thompson

b. Stephen Curry

c. Draymond Green

d. Andre Iguodala

4. Who is the Warriors' all-time leader in assists?

a. Chris Mullin

b. Stephen Curry

c. Tim Hardaway

d. Rick Barry

5. In which season did the Warriors first wear their "We Believe" jerseys?

a. 2005-2006

b. 2006-2007

c. 2007-2008

d. 2008-2009

6. Which player was traded from the Warriors to the Dallas Mavericks in 2024?

a. Kevin Durant

b. Stephen Curry

c. DeMarcus Cousins

d. Klay Thompson

7. Which former Warrior was part of the original "Run TMC" trio?

a. Chris Mullin

b. Tim Hardaway

c. Mitch Richmond

d. All of the above

8. What was the Warriors' slogan during the 2015 championship run?

a. Strength in Numbers

b. We Believe

c. The Future is Bright

d. The Return of the Warriors

9. Who was the Warriors' first head coach?

a. Frank McGuire

b. Alex Hannum

c. Bill Sharman

d. Eddie Gottlieb   .

10. In which year did the Golden State Warriors retire Al Attles' jersey number 16?

a. 1970

b. 1972

c. 1973

d. 1977

11. Who was the Warriors' head coach before Steve Kerr?

a. Keith Smart

b. Don Nelson

c. Mark Jackson

d. Mike Montgomery

12. Who was the starting Shooting Guard on the Warriors in 2023?

a. Brandin Podziemski

b. Andrew Wiggins

c. Jonathan Kuminga

d. Draymond Green

13. Which year did the Warriors sign Harvard guard Jeremy Lin on a two-year deal?

a. 2009

b. 2010

c. 2011

d. 2012

ABOUT THE AUTHOR

John Stevenson is a Michigan-based author of children's sports books. He is the father of two children, James and Tracy. When not writing new books, John can be found playing sports with his family or going on road trips. Through his books, John hopes to empower young readers and spark their imagination.

ENJOYED THE BOOK?

I'd really appreciate it if you could leave a review on Amazon. The number of reviews a book receives helps more people discover it. Even a short review can make a big difference, allowing me to keep doing what I love. Thank you in advance!

Trivia Answers

1. Cleveland Cavaliers **2.** Blue and gold **3.** Andre Iguodala **4.** Stephen Curry **5.** 2006-2007 **6.** Klay Thompson **7.** All of the above **8.** Strength in Numbers **9.** Eddie Gottlieb **10.** 1977 **11.** Mark Jackson **12.** Brandin Podziemski **13.** 2010